Gorgeous friends,

This year we're stepping up from milk, cookies and a nip of whiskey by the tree.

I'm coming in hot to light up the holidays like never before.

Yours Lit,

Jolly St Nick.

# Contents

SHOTS:



BOURBON:



GIN:

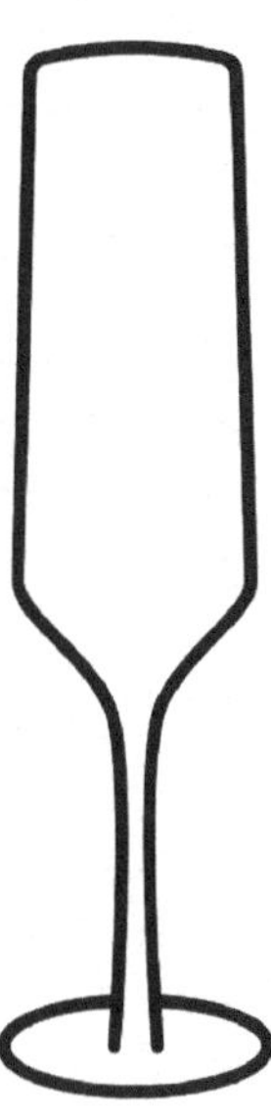

# BRING ON THE SHOTS

# Christmas Kamikaze

**Ingredients:**
1/2 oz vodka, 1/2 oz triple sec, splash of lime juice, splash of cranberry juice.

**Directions:**
Shake all ingredients with ice and strain into a shot glass.

# Frosty Lemon Drop

**Ingredients:**
1/2 oz vanilla vodka, 1/2 oz lemon juice, sugar rim, a hint of peppermint extract.

**Directions:**
Rim the shot glass with sugar. Shake vodka, lemon juice, and peppermint extract with ice. Strain into the prepared glass.

# Very Merry Mule

**Ingredients:**
1/2 oz vodka, 1/2 oz ginger beer, a squeeze of lime, a splash of peppermint schnapps.

**Directions:**
Combine vodka, ginger beer, lime juice, and peppermint schnapps in a shaker with ice, shake and strain into a shot glass.

# Irish Sleigh Bomb

**Ingredients:**

1/2 pint stout beer, 1/2 oz Irish Bourbon, 1/2 oz Irish cream, a dash of cinnamon.

**Directions:**

Pour stout into a glass. Mix Bourbon and Irish cream in a shot glass, add a dash of cinnamon, and drop the shot glass into the stout before drinking.

# Christmas Fireball

**Ingredients:**

1 oz cinnamon Bourbon, a splash of hot apple cider.

**Directions:**

Mix cinnamon Bourbon with hot apple cider in a shot glass.

# Santa Sour

**Ingredients:**

1/2 oz Bourbon, 1/2 oz lemon juice, 1/2 oz maple syrup, dash of nutmeg.

**Directions:**

Combine Bourbon, lemon juice, and maple syrup in a shaker with ice. Shake well and strain into a shot glass.

# The Candy Cane

**Ingredients:**
1/2 oz peppermint schnapps, 1/2 oz white chocolate liqueur.

**Directions:**
Mix the peppermint schnapps and white chocolate liqueur in a shaker with ice. Strain into a shot glass.

# Mistletoe Madness

**Ingredients:**
1/2 oz green crème de menthe, 1/2 oz cherry liqueur.

**Directions:**
Pour the green crème de menthe into a shot glass, then slowly layer the cherry liqueur on top.

# Frosty the Snowman

**Ingredients:**
1/2 oz vanilla vodka, 1/2 oz blue curaçao, a splash of lemon-lime soda.

**Directions:**
Mix the vanilla vodka and blue curaçao in a shaker with ice. Strain into a shot glass and top with a splash of lemon-lime soda.

## Merry Margarita

**Ingredients:**
1/2 oz tequila, 1/4 oz triple sec, 1/4 oz lime juice, a splash of cranberry juice for color.

**Directions:**
Shake the tequila, triple sec, lime juice, and cranberry juice with ice. Strain **into a shot glass.**

## Santas Little Helper

**Ingredients:**
1/2 oz tequila, 1/2 oz peppermint schnapps.

**Directions:**
Pour the tequila into a shot glass, followed by the peppermint schnapps for a minty kick.

## Rudolphs Revenge

**Ingredients:**
1/2 oz tequila, 1/2 oz coffee liqueur, a dash of chili powder.

**Directions:**
Shake the tequila and coffee liqueur with ice, strain into a shot glass, and add a dash of chili powder on top.

# Things youll need:

Knife / Chopping Board
Juicer
Blender
Mini Skewers
Muddler
Lots of Ice
Sugar
Salt
Spices

# bourbon

# bourbon

## Classic Christmas Eggnog

Eggnog originated in medieval Britain. It evolved from "posset," a hot, milky, ale-like drink. By the 13th century, monks were known to drink a posset with eggs and figs. Over time, this drink became part of the Christmas tradition, especially in England, where it was popular among the aristocracy due to the cost of milk, eggs, and sherry. The beverage crossed the Atlantic to the American colonies, where it became tied to the holiday season. George Washington even had his own famous recipe. Eggnog is traditionally made with milk, cream, sugar, whipped eggs, and spirits such as brandy, rum, or Bourbon, and it continues to be a festive favorite, embodying the spirit of holiday indulgence and cheer.

---

- 6 EGGS
- 3/4 cup SUGAR
- 2 cups MILK
- 1 cup HEAVY CREAM
- 1 cup BOURBON
- 1/4 tsp VANILLA EXTRACT
- NUTMEG

---

SERVES 4: Separate the eggs, placing the yolks in one bowl and the whites in another. Cover the whites and refrigerate until needed. Beat the yolks with the sugar until the mixture is light and creamy. Stir in the milk, cream, Bourbon nutmeg, and vanilla extract into the yolk mixture. Cover the yolk mixture and refrigerate for at least 1 hour. The longer it chills, the more the flavors will meld together.

Just before serving, beat the egg whites in a separate bowl to soft peaks. Gently fold the beaten egg whites into the chilled yolk mixture. Pour eggnog into a punch bowl or pitcher. Grate fresh nutmeg on top for garnish and serve in brandy snifters or mugs.

# bourbon

## Christmas Old Fashioned

The Old Fashioned, a revered American classic, traces its origins to the early 19th century. It gained its name and fame at the Pendennis Club in Louisville, Kentucky, in the 1880s, where it was concocted for Colonel James E. Pepper, a notable Bourbon distiller. Pepper then introduced the drink to the elite at the Waldorf-Astoria Hotel in New York City. Characterized by its simplicity, the Old Fashioned combines Bourbon with sugar, water, and bitters, epitomizing the elegance of minimalism in cocktails. Despite its variations over the years, the Old Fashioned remains a symbol of timeless sophistication.

---

| | |
|---|---|
| 2 oz BOURBON | ORANGE PEEL |
| 1 SUGAR CUBE | CRANBERRIES |
| ANGOSTURA BITTERS | ROSEMARY SPRIG |

---

Muddle the sugar cube and bitters with one bar spoon of water at the bottom of a glass. Fill the glass with 1 to 2 large ice cubes, add the Bourbon, and gently stir to combine. Express the oil of an orange peel over the glass, then drop in. Garnish with cranberries and a rosemary sprig to add the festive touch.

# bourbon

## Winter Bourbon Sour

The Bourbon Sour, a classic cocktail with a harmonious blend of tart and sweet, has its roots in the late 18th century. Originally developed as a means to make rough spirits more palatable, it was formalized in the 1862 bartender's guide by Jerry Thomas. The drink gained widespread popularity in the 19th and 20th centuries, especially among sailors who used it to prevent scurvy, thanks to its vitamin C-rich lemon juice. Comprising Bourbon, lemon juice, and sugar, the Bourbon Sour has endured through the ages, evolving with various twists but always maintaining its core identity as a beloved staple in the cocktail world.

---

2 oz BOURBON

3/4 oz LEMON JUICE

1/2 oz MAPLE SYRUP

1/2 oz ORANGE LIQUEUR

ORANGE ZEST

CINNAMON STICK

---

Combine Bourbon, lemon juice, maple syrup, and orange liqueur in a shaker with ice. Shake until cold and strain into a rocks glass filled with ice. Garnish with orange zest and a cinnamon stick. Sugar rim optional.

# bourbon

## Merry Mint Julep

The Mint Julep, an iconic Southern cocktail, boasts a history that stretches back to the 18th century. Originally a medicinal concoction used for its stomach-soothing properties, it evolved into a symbol of Southern hospitality and leisure. The drink gained prominence in the American South, particularly in Kentucky, where it became closely associated with the Kentucky Derby in the 20th century. Traditionally made with Bourbon, sugar, water, and fresh mint, served over crushed ice in a silver or pewter cup, the Mint Julep is much more than a drink — it's a cultural emblem, representing the charm and traditions of the South.

---

2 oz BOURBON

1 oz CRANBERRY JUICE

1/2 oz SIMPLE SYRUP

MINT LEAVES

CRUSHED ICE

SPRIG OF ROSEMARY

---

In a julep cup gently muddle the mint leaves with the simple syrup. Be careful not to shred the mint, as you only want to release the oils. Pour in the Bourbon and cranberry juice over the muddled mint. Fill the cup with crushed ice up to the brim. Stir the mixture gently until the cup becomes frosty. Garnish with a few fresh cranberries and a sprig of rosemary.

# bourbon

## Hottest Hot Toddy

The Hot Toddy, a warm and soothing cocktail, has origins dating back to 18th-century Scotland. Initially the Hot Toddy was concocted as a remedy for cold weather ailments. The inclusion of spices and citrus, often believed to have medicinal benefits, made it popular in cold climates and among those seeking relief from the flu or cold. Over time, the Hot Toddy transcended its medicinal roots, becoming a beloved winter beverage. Known for its warmth and comfort, it embodies the essence of a cozy evening, making it a staple in cold-weather cocktail menus worldwide.

---

2 oz BOURBON

1 tsp HONEY

4 oz HOT WATER

2 tsp LEMON JUICE

CINNAMON STICK

2 CLOVES

LEMON SLICE

SPRIG OF ROSEMARY

---

Warm your mug with hot water first, then empty it. This helps to keep your drink warm for a longer time. In the warmed mug, combine the Bourbon, honey, and lemon juice. Pour the hot water and stir well with the cinnamon stick until the honey is fully dissolved. Add the cloves, a lemon slice and a sprig of rosemary for garnish and flavor.

# bourbon

## Mistletoe Manhattan

The Manhattan cocktail originated in the late 19th century in New York City. Its creation is often attributed to a banquet hosted by Winston Churchill's mother, Lady Randolph Churchill, at the Manhattan Club in the early 1870s. However, this story is widely considered a myth, as Lady Churchill was likely in France at the time. The true origins of the Manhattan are unclear, but its first documented recipe appeared in O.H. Byron's 1884 book "The Modern Bartender." The Manhattan, traditionally made with Bourbon, sweet vermouth, and bitters, quickly gained popularity and has since become a staple in bars worldwide, known for its sophistication and versatility in variations.

---

- 2 oz BOURBON
- 1 oz VERMOUTH
- 1/2 oz CINNAMON SYRUP
- MARASCHINO CHERRY
- ANGOSTURA BITTERS
- ORANGE PEEL
- SPRIG ROSEMARY

---

Firstly, for the Cinnamon Syrup, you can make this by simmering equal parts water and sugar with a few cinnamon sticks until nice and sticky. Place your cocktail glass in the freezer for a few minutes to chill. In a mixing glass, combine the Bourbon, vermouth, cinnamon syrup, and a few dashes of Angostura bitters. Fill the mixing glass with ice. Stir the mixture for about 30 seconds to properly chill and dilute the cocktail. To garnish, twist the orange peel over the cocktail to release its oils, then drop it into the glass. Add the maraschino cherry. Strain the cocktail into the chilled glass.

# bourbon

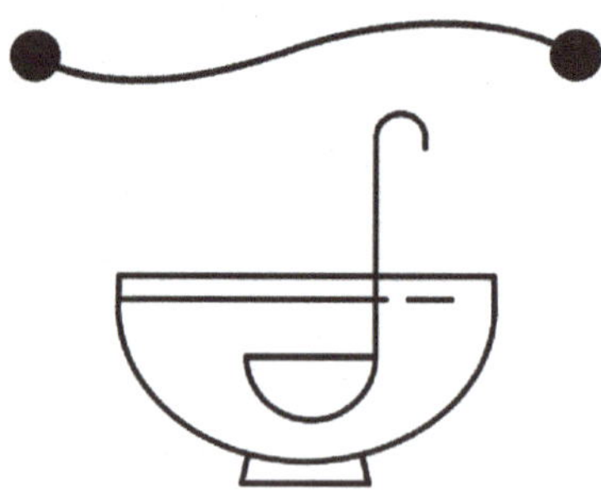

## Very Hard & Very Spiced Apple Cider

Spiced Apple Cider has roots tracing back to colonial America. Apple cider was a common drink due to the abundance of apple orchards and the simplicity of cider-making. The practice of mulling cider with spices like cinnamon, cloves, and allspice likely originated from Europe's tradition of mulled wine. As settlers in America adapted their recipes to local ingredients, spiced apple cider emerged as a popular drink, especially in the fall and winter. Today, spiced apple cider is synonymous with autumn and winter festivities, embodying the warmth and comfort of the season and often enjoyed during holiday celebrations and gatherings.

---

1 gal APPLE CIDER

2 cups BOURBON

1 ORANGE

4 CINNAMON STICKS

1 tsp WHOLE CLOVES

1 tbs ALLSPICE BERRIES

---

MAKES +12 CUPS: In a large pot, combine the apple cider with the orange slices, cinnamon sticks, whole cloves, and allspice berries. If you have one, use a spice bag or cheesecloth for the spices as it makes removal easier. Heat at medium just until it begins to simmer. Then, reduce the heat to low. Avoid boiling to keep the flavors fresh and vibrant. Let the cider simmer gently for about 30 minutes to allow the spices to infuse their flavors. The longer you simmer, the more pronounced the spice flavors will be. Stir in the rum or Bourbon after removing the cider from the heat. Strain out the spices and orange slices. Ladle the hot cider into mugs and garnish with a cinnamon stick and orange slice.

# GIN

## A Very Merry Martini

The Martini originated in the United States in the late 19th century. Some trace it back to the "Martinez" cocktail from Martinez, California, while others link it to the Occidental Hotel in San Francisco. The Martini evolved from a mix of gin, vermouth, and various bitters into the more streamlined gin and dry vermouth concoction known today. Gaining immense popularity during the Prohibition era, the Martini has become a symbol of sophistication, undergoing various adaptations including the rise of the dirty, vodka & espresso Martinis, yet it remains a quintessential staple in the world of mixology.

---

| | |
|---|---|
| 2 oz GIN | SPRIG OF ROSEMARY |
| 1/2 oz VERMOUTH | BLACK PEPPERCORNS |
| SPRIG OF THYME | LEMON PEEL |

---

For any Martini, always ensure Gin is always stored in the freezer so its texture is velvety upon pouring. Lightly muddle the thyme and rosemary in the bottom of a mixing glass to release their oils. Add the black peppercorns. Pour in the gin and dry vermouth over the herbs and peppercorns. Fill mixing glass with ice and shake/stir the mixture well until it is thoroughly chilled. Strain the mixture into a chilled martini glass, ensuring that the herbs and peppercorns are left behind. Garnish with rosemary and a twisted strip of lemon.

# GIN

## NOEL NEGRONI

The Negroni boasts a history dating back to the early 20th century. Its creation is commonly attributed to Count Camillo Negroni in Florence around 1919, who asked the bartender to strengthen his favorite cocktail, the Americano, by replacing the soda water with gin. The bartender also added an orange garnish, instead of the typical lemon of the Americano, to signify the new drink. Comprising equal parts of gin, sweet vermouth, and Campari, a bitter Italian aperitif, the Negroni has a distinctively bold and balanced flavor. Its popularity has surged globally, inspiring a myriad of variations. The cocktail's simple yet sophisticated profile has made it a beloved classic in bars and restaurants worldwide.

---

1 oz GIN

1 oz CAMPARI

1 oz SWEET VERMOUTH

ORANGE PEEL

CINNAMON STICK

---

In a mixing glass, combine gin, vermouth, and Campari over ice. Stir the mixture until well chilled, about 20 seconds. Strain into a chilled rocks glass with a large ice cube. Squeeze the orange peel over the drink to release its oils, then place it in the glass along with the cinnamon stick for garnish and extra festive flavor.

# GIN

## Frosted Gin Fizz

The Gin Fizz is a classic cocktail that is part of the fizz family, a group of mixed drinks that are similar to sours but with the addition of a carbonated water. It dates back to the 19th century, with its first recorded mention in the 1876 edition of Jerry Thomas' "Bartender's Guide." As one of the most iconic examples of a fizz, the Gin Fizz became extremely popular in America, particularly in New Orleans, which is often considered its spiritual home. The traditional Gin Fizz blends gin with lemon juice, sugar, and soda water, shaken into a frothy delight and served over ice. It's celebrated for its refreshing and effervescent qualities, making it a beloved choice, especially during the summer months.

---

2 oz GIN

1 oz LEMON JUICE

1/2 oz SIMPLE SYRUP

2 oz CLUB SODA

1 EGG WHITE

POMEGRANATE SEEDS

---

Begin by placing your glass (sidecar or tumbler) in the freezer to chill. A frosted glass will keep your fizz cool and refreshing. Start by adding the gin, lemon juice, simple syrup, and egg white to a shaker. Shake vigorously without ice - this is known as a dry shake - to emulsify the egg white. After the dry shake, add a handful of ice to the shaker and shake again. This second shake chills the drink and adds a silky-smooth froth. Take your chilled glass and strain the mixture into it. Top off with soda water to give it that characteristic fizz. Sprinkle a few pomegranate seeds over the froth and the festive flare.

# GIN

## Christmas Gin & Tonic

The Gin and Tonic has its origins in the days of the British Empire in India. British officers took to adding a splash of gin to the quinine tonic they drank to ward off malaria, improving its bitter taste. Quinine, derived from the bark of the cinchona tree, was an effective anti-malarial prophylactic. In the 19th century, this practical concoction became a pleasurable beverage with the addition of lime to balance the bitterness. The Gin and Tonic, with its crisp and refreshing profile, quickly grew in popularity. It went on to become a staple drink, not just in tropical regions but also as a classic cocktail enjoyed worldwide.

---

2 oz GIN

4 oz TONIC

1/4 oz LIME JUICE

1/4 oz ROSEMARY SYRUP

SPRIG ROSEMARY

ORANGE PEEL

---

Ahead of time, make your rosemary simple syrup by simmering equal parts sugar and water with a couple of sprigs of rosemary until the sugar dissolves. Allow it to cool.

Start by chilling your highball glass in the freezer to keep the drink crisp. Combine the gin with the rosemary simple syrup and fresh lime juice. Fill the glass with large ice cubes, which melt slower and keep your drink colder for longer without diluting it. Pour the tonic water over the gin mixture gently - you want to maintain its effervescence. Stir the drink gently to mix. Garnish with a sprig of rosemary and an orange peel.

# GIN

## A Festive French 75

The French 75, has roots dating back to World War I. Its name is a nod to the 75mm field gun used by the French military, reputed for its precision and rapid fire, much like the cocktail's sharp and strong delivery. The drink was first crafted at Harry's New York Bar in Paris around 1915 by barman Harry MacElhone. The original recipe called for a mix of gin, lemon juice, two dashes of simple syrup, and finished with Champagne. This concoction was said to have such a kick that it felt like being shelled by the rapid-firing French 75 field gun. Over time, the French 75 has become a celebratory beverage, synonymous with elegance and refinement, and it remains a popular choice for toasts and special occasions.

---

1 oz GIN

1/2 oz LEMON JUICE

1/2 oz SIMPLE SYRUP

3 oz CHAMPAGNE

LEMON PEEL

---

Place the champagne flute in the freezer for a short time to ensure your cocktail stays crisp. In a cocktail shaker, combine the gin, lemon juice, and simple syrup with ice, shaking until the outside of the shaker feels cold. Remove the flute from the chiller and strain the shaker contents into it, leaving enough room for the Champagne. Gently pour the over the back of a spoon onto the gin mixture to maintain the bubbly texture. Twist a strip of lemon peel over the cocktail to express its oils, then run it around the rim of the glass before dropping it in.

# VODKA

# VODKA

## Gingerbread Espresso Martini

The Espresso Martini, a modern classic, was created in the 1980s by London bartender Dick Bradsell. Bradsell developed this invigorating concoction at the Soho Brasserie in response to a model's request for a drink that would both perk her up and be intoxicating. Combining vodka, fresh espresso, coffee liqueur, and sugar, the Espresso Martini quickly garnered acclaim for its bold flavor and energizing effect. It rose to prominence during the 1990s cocktail renaissance and remains a beloved staple in the world of mixology.

---

- 2 oz VODKA
- 1/2 oz KAHLUA
- 1 oz ESPRESSO
- 1/4 oz GINGERBREAD SYRUP
- GROUND NUTMEG
- COFFEE BEANS

---

Before you get started: Brew a strong espresso and allow it to cool. For the gingerbread syrup: simmer water, sugar, and spices until it reduces into a syrupy consistency, then let it cool. Also, don't forget to place your martini glass in the freezer to chill.

To start the cocktail, in a shaker, add the vodka, Kahlua, espresso, and gingerbread syrup. Fill the shaker with ice and shake vigorously. The goal is to chill the liquid and create a nice froth from the espresso. Strain the mixture into the chilled martini glass. The coffee should create a lovely crema on top. Sprinkle a touch of ground nutmeg or cinnamon over the crema for a festive spice aroma. Place three coffee beans in the center for the classic espresso martini look.

# VODKA

## Bloody Merry

The Bloody Mary dates back to the 1920s or 1930s. The drink is often attributed to Fernand Petiot, a bartender at Harry's New York Bar in Paris, who later refined the recipe at the St. Regis Hotel in New York City. Initially, the cocktail was a simple blend of vodka and tomato juice, but Petiot added seasonings like salt, pepper, lemon, Worcestershire sauce, and Tabasco to create the complex flavor profile we know today. The origin of the name "Bloody Mary" is equally enigmatic, with theories ranging from it being named after Queen Mary I of England to a patron at Petiot's bar. Over the decades, the Bloody Mary has evolved into a brunch staple and a popular hangover cure, famous for its versatility and the countless variations it has inspired in bars around the world.

---

- 2 oz VODKA
- 4 oz TOMATO JUICE
- 1/2 oz LEMON JUICE
- 1/2 tsp HORSERADISH
- 2 dashes WORCESTERSHIRE
- 1 dash TABASCO
- 1/2 tsp PAPRIKA
- FRESH HERBS*
- GARNISH**

---

Rim a tall glass with a mixture of salt and smoked paprika. Fill the glass with ice. In a shaker, combine the vodka, tomato juice, lemon juice, horseradish, Worcestershire sauce, hot sauce, smoked paprika, and chopped herbs (*Thyme / Rosemary). Shake the mixture well to ensure all the flavors are well blended. Taste and adjust the seasoning with salt and pepper. Strain the mixture into the prepared glass over the ice. **Garnish with a celery stick, a cranberry, a skewer of green olives and red bell pepper pieces..

# VODKA

## Merry Moscow Mule

The Moscow Mule was created in the 1940s in the United States. Its invention is often attributed to John G. Martin, an executive at the spirits company Heublein, and Jack Morgan, the owner of the Cock 'n' Bull pub in Los Angeles. The story goes that Martin, struggling to sell his newly acquired brand of vodka, and Morgan, looking to offload an excess stock of ginger beer, together concocted this refreshing beverage. The addition of lime juice and the presentation in a copper mug, which was a marketing strategy to make the drink stand out, completed the creation. The Moscow Mule played a significant role in popularizing vodka in the United States, transitioning it from a relatively unknown spirit to one of the most consumed liquors.

---

2 oz VODKA

4 oz GINGER BEER

1/2 oz LIME JUICE

1/4 cup POM JUICE

POM SEEDS

ROSEMARY SPRIG

---

Fill a copper mug with ice and pour the vodka, lime juice, and pomegranate juice. Top the beverage with ginger beer and garnish with a few pomegranate seeds, a lime wedge, and a sprig of rosemary for a hint of color and a festive feeling.

# VODKA

## Peppermint White Russian

The White Russian emerged in the mid-20th century and is believed to be an evolution of the Black Russian, a simple mixture of vodka and coffee liqueur. The Black Russian was created in the late 1940s by bartender Gustave Tops at the Hotel Metropole in Brussels, Belgium, in honor of the U.S. ambassador to Luxembourg. The addition of cream transformed it into the White Russian, which is thought to have occurred in the 1960s. Despite its name, the drink has no direct connection to Russia. The White Russian gained significant popularity in the late 1990s, particularly in the United States, largely due to its prominent role in the film "The Big Lebowski." Its rich, sweet, and accessible flavor profile has made it a favorite among creamy cocktail lovers.

---

2 oz VODKA

1 oz HEAVY CREAM

1 oz KAHLUA

CANDY CANES

1/2 oz PEPPERMINT SCHNAPPS

---

Rim a rocks glass with crushed candy canes (optional). To do this, moisten the rim with a little coffee liqueur, then dip it into the crushed candy. Fill the glass with ice. Pour the vodka, Kahlua and peppermint schnapps over the ice in the glass, mix gently. Slowly pour the heavy cream over the back of a spoon into the glass to create a layered effect. Adjust the amount of cream according to your preference & add a candy cane for garnish.

# TEQUILA

# & RUM

# TEQUILA

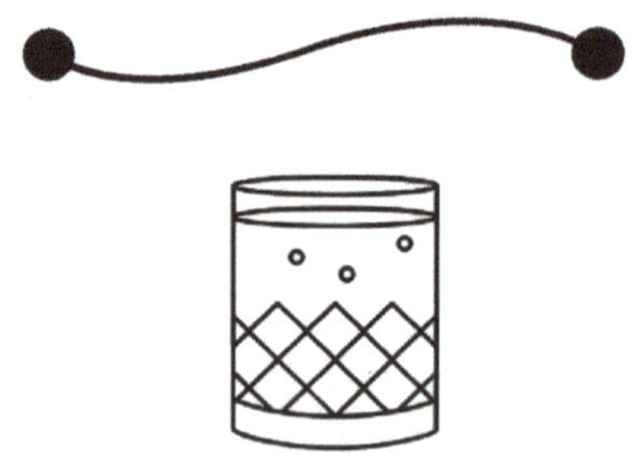

## CHRISTMAS CRANBERRY MARGARITA

The Margarita has a history shrouded in mystery and multiple origin stories. The most commonly accepted narrative traces its origins back to the 1930s or 1940s in Mexico. One popular tale credits Carlos "Danny" Herrera, a Mexican bartender, who created the drink in 1938 at his Tijuana-area restaurant, Rancho La Gloria, for a customer allergic to all spirits except tequila. Another account attributes the invention to Margarita Sames, a wealthy Dallas socialite, who purportedly mixed the drink for her guests at her Acapulco vacation home in 1948. Regardless of its true origins, the Margarita, gained popularity in the 1950s and has since become synonymous with Mexican cuisine and culture, often enjoyed in various forms, from classic on the rocks to frozen variations.

---

2 oz TEQUILA

1 oz COINTREAU

1 oz FRESH LIME JUICE

1 oz CRANBERRY JUICE

1/2 oz AGAVE

RIM SALT or SUGAR

LIME SLICES

---

Start by rimming your glass with lime juice and then dipping it in either salt or sugar, based on your preference. This adds a decorative touch and extra flavor. In a shaker, combine the tequila, triple sec, lime juice, cranberry juice, and agave (or simple syrup). Fill the shaker with ice and shake vigorously for about 15 seconds. Shaking not only chills the drink but also properly integrates all the flavors. Strain the mixture into the prepared glass filled with ice. A fine strain can be used to remove small ice chips and pulp. Garnish the drink with a few fresh cranberries and a slice of lime on the rim or floating in the drink.

# TEQUILA

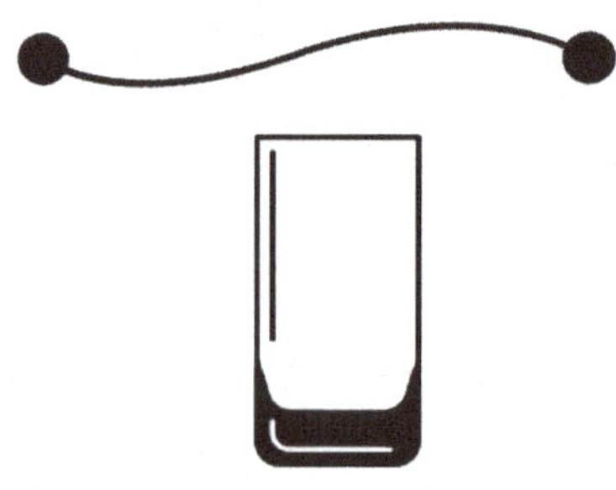

## WINTER PALOMA

The Paloma origins, while not precisely documented, are widely believed to be in Mexico, likely emerging sometime after the introduction of grapefruit, which arrived in the country in the early 20th century. The Paloma, Spanish for "dove," is traditionally made with tequila and grapefruit soda, often enhanced with lime juice and served on the rocks with a salted rim. Its simplicity and the balance of sweet and tart flavors have made it a popular choice, often overshadowing the Margarita in Mexico. The Paloma's rise in popularity is recent, coinciding with the growing international appreciation of tequila and the cocktail's refreshing profile, making it a staple in bars worldwide and a symbol of contemporary Mexican culture.

---

2 oz TEQUILA

1/2 oz FRESH LIME JUICE

4 oz GRAPEFRUIT JUICE

1/2 oz ROSEMARY SYRUP

GRAPEFRUIT

CLUB SODA

---

For a homemade rosemary syrup, simmer equal parts water and sugar with a few sprigs of rosemary or a couple of cinnamon sticks until the sugar dissolves. Allow it to cool before using. In a shaker, combine the tequila, grapefruit juice, lime juice, and rosemary syrup. Add ice to the shaker and shake well for about 15 seconds. Shaking helps blend the flavors and chill the drink. Fill a highball glass with ice and strain the mixture into the prepared glass. Gently top the drink with soda water which will a refreshing fizz to the cocktail. Garnish with a sprig of rosemary and a slice of grapefruit.

# Rum

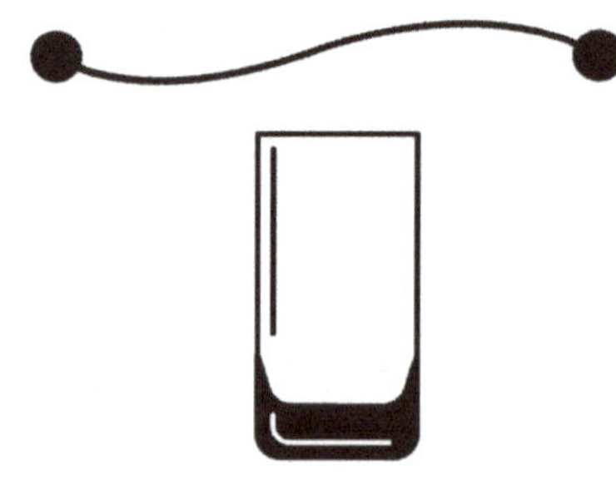

## Pomegranate & Mint Mojito

The Mojito, a refreshing cocktail synonymous with Cuban culture, traces its lineage back to the 16th century "El Draque," a medicinal mix of aguardiente, sugar, lime, and mint. As rum distillation evolved, so did the Mojito, adopting white rum in place of aguardiente. The drink became a staple in Havana's vibrant social scene, a favorite among locals and luminaries alike, including the famed writer Ernest Hemingway. Renowned for its invigorating blend of sweetness, citrus zest, and minty freshness, the Mojito has cemented its status as a beloved cocktail enjoyed around the globe.

---

2 oz WHITE RUM

1 oz POMEGRANATE JUICE

1 oz SIMPLE SYRUP

1 oz LIME JUICE

CLUB SODA

POM SEEDS / MINT LEAVES

---

In a sturdy glass, gently muddle a handful of mint leaves with the simple syrup and lime juice. This releases the oils from the mint and combines them with the sweet and sour components. Pour in the pomegranate juice and the white rum. Add the ice cubes to the glass, filling it to near the top. Pour soda water over the ice to fill the glass, leaving just a bit of room for the garnishes. Sprinkle a spoonful of pomegranate seeds over the top for garnish.

# Rum

## I LIKE CHRISTMAS COLADAS

The Piña Colada has its roots in Puerto Rico. The drink's name means "strained pineapple" in Spanish, a reference to its key ingredient. Its origin is commonly attributed to a bartender named Ramón "Monchito" Marrero at the Caribe Hilton in San Juan, who in 1954 set out to capture the flavors of the island in a glass. After months of experimentation, Marrero blended coconut cream, pineapple juice, and white rum to create what would become Puerto Rico's national drink. The Piña Colada was further popularized by the song "Escape" (The Piña Colada Song) in 1979, and since then, its fame has spread worldwide, becoming a symbol of beach vacations and laid-back living.

| | | |
|---|---|---|
| 3 oz COCONUT RUM | 2 oz COCONUT CREAM | pinch GROUND CLOVE |
| 1 oz SPICED RUM | 1/4 tsp VANILLA EXT. | pinch GROUND GINGER |
| 4 oz PINEAPPLE JUICE | 1/4 tsp CINNAMON | GARNISHES* |

In a blender, combine the coconut rum, spiced rum, pineapple juice, coconut cream, vanilla extract, ground cinnamon, clove, and ginger. Add a generous amount of ice and blend the mixture until it's smooth and creamy. If desired, rim your glass with a mixture of cinnamon and sugar for an extra festive touch. Pour the blended mixture into a chilled glass. Top with a dollop of whipped cream. *Garnish with a dollop of whipped cream, a cinnamon stick, a slice of pineapple, and a maraschino cherry.

# Rum

## Pumpkin Pie Martini

Pumpkin pie, an emblem of American Thanksgiving and autumn, originated from early European settlers in North America who adapted Native American uses of pumpkins. Initially, pumpkins were filled with milk, honey, and spices, and baked in hot ashes. By the 17th century, recipes evolved in English cookbooks towards the crust-based pies we recognize today. The pie gained iconic status in the 19th century, especially in relation to Thanksgiving, solidifying its place as a symbol of American tradition and harvest celebrations. Now, pumpkin pie is a quintessential element of American fall and holiday cuisine, cherished for its creamy texture and warm spices.

---

| | | |
|---|---|---|
| 2 oz SPICED RUM | 1/2 oz MAPLE SYRUP | pinch CINNAMON |
| 1 oz PUMPKIN PUREE | 1/4 tsp VANILLA EXT. | pinch GINGER |
| 1/2 oz HEAVY CREAM | pinch NUTMEG | GARNISHES* |

---

Prepare the Glass (Optional): If you'd like a graham cracker rim, moisten the rim of a martini glass with maple syrup or water and dip it into crushed graham crackers. In a shaker, combine the spiced rum, pumpkin puree, heavy cream, vanilla extract, maple syrup, cinnamon, nutmeg, and ginger. Add ice to the shaker and shake vigorously. The shaking will chill the drink and help blend the pumpkin puree smoothly with the other ingredients. Strain the mixture into the prepared martini glass. *Garnish with a cinnamon stick. If desired, add a dollop of whipped cream on top for an extra indulgent treat.

# Rum

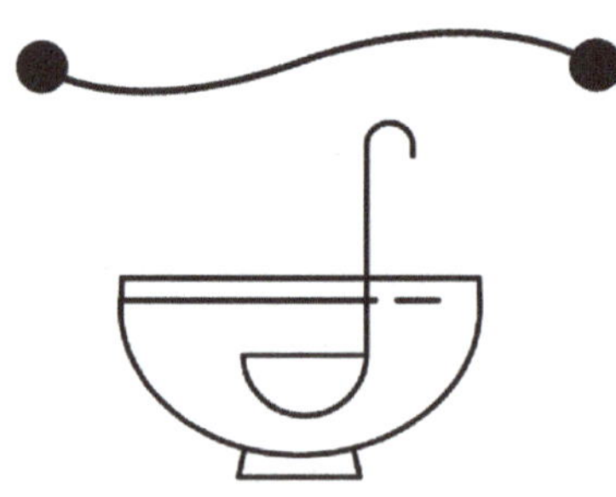

## Rudolph's Rum Punch

Rum Punch traces its origins back to the 17th century in the Caribbean. The introduction of rum to the Caribbean by European colonists and the subsequent establishment of sugar plantations led to the creation of this iconic drink. Rum, abundant and cheap, was mixed with citrus juice to prevent scurvy among sailors, and with sugar and spices to enhance its flavor, giving birth to the early versions of Rum Punch. The drink became a staple in the Caribbean and was later popularized in colonial America and England. The basic formula, often remembered by the rhyme "One of Sour, Two of Sweet, Three of Strong, Four of Weak," underscores its simplicity and adaptability.

---

| | | |
|---|---|---|
| 3 cups DARK RUM | 2 cups ORANGE JUICE | 1 ltr GINGER ALE |
| 1 cup LIGHT RUM | 1 cup PINEAPPLE JUICE | FRUIT ASSORTMENT |
| 1/2 cup LIME JUICE | 1/4 cup GRENADINE | CINNAMON STICKS |

---

In a large punch bowl, combine the dark rum, light rum, orange juice, pineapple juice, and lime juice. Pour in the grenadine, which will give the punch a beautiful red hue and a touch of sweetness. Refrigerate the mixture for at least 1 hour to allow the flavors to meld together. Just before serving, add ginger ale (or sub for club soda) as well as the fruit — which you can choose based on preference and seasonality / availability. Examples - orange slices, lime slices, maraschino cherries, pineapple, watermelon, strawberries, etc. Optionally, garnish with cinnamon sticks for a festive feel.

# BUBBLES & VINO

# BUBBLES

## Classic Campari Spritz

The Campari Spritz, a staple of Italian aperitif culture, has its origins in the Veneto region of Italy. Its history dates back to the 1800s when Austro-Hungarian soldiers in the region diluted local wines with water, a practice that evolved into the spritz. The addition of Campari, created in 1860 by Gaspare Campari in Milan, to this mix of wine and soda water in the early 20th century transformed the spritz into the vibrant and bittersweet cocktail known today. Emblematic of Italian lifestyle and leisure, the Campari Spritz has gained global popularity, symbolizing the joy of socializing and the art of the aperitif.

---

2 oz CAMPARI

1 oz CLUB SODA

3 ox PROSECCO

ORANGE SLICE

---

Fill a large wine glass with ice cubes to keep the drink cold and well-diluted. Pour the Campari over the ice. Gently pour the prosecco into the glass and top with soda. Garnish with a slice of orange. Sub Campari for Aperol if you prefer a sweeter cocktail.

# Christmas Morning Bellini

The Bellini was born in the mid-20th century at Harry's Bar in Venice, Italy, a favorite haunt of Ernest Hemingway, Sinclair Lewis, and Orson Welles. Created by Giuseppe Cipriani, the founder of Harry's Bar, the Bellini's inception was around 1948. Cipriani was inspired by the region's abundant white peaches and the 15th-century Venetian artist Giovanni Bellini, from whom the drink takes its name. The original recipe was a simple, yet elegant blend of puréed white peaches and Prosecco, an Italian sparkling wine. The Bellini quickly became a symbol of the sophisticated and luxurious Venetian lifestyle and has since gained international acclaim, becoming a staple in bars and brunch tables worldwide.

---

2 oz PEACH PUREE

4 ox PROSECCO

RASPBERRY LIQUEUR

RASPBERRIES & MINT

---

Prepare the Purée: If you're using fresh peaches, blend them into a smooth purée. If peaches are out of season, good quality peach nectar works just as well. In a champagne flute, combine the peach purée or nectar with a splash of raspberry liqueur. The raspberry adds a hint of tartness and also gives the drink a festive, rosy hue. Gently pour the chilled Prosecco over the peach and raspberry mixture. Pouring slowly helps to keep the bubbly fizz. Drop a few fresh raspberries into the flute, which will float beautifully on top, and add a small sprig of mint for a pop of green that's both aromatic and Christmassy.

# Vino

## Christmas Sangria

Sangria has its origins in Spain and Portugal. Its roots can be traced back to the Roman Empire when Romans planted vineyards and often mixed wine with water and herbs to make it safer to drink. The term "sangria" is derived from the Spanish word "sangre," meaning blood, referring to its typical deep red color from red wine. It gained international recognition at the 1964 New York World's Fair, where it was served at the Spanish Pavilion. This refreshing beverage typically combines red wine with fresh fruit, a sweetener, and a small amount of brandy or another spirit. Over time, numerous variations of sangria have emerged, adapting to local tastes and seasonal ingredients, making it a versatile and beloved drink around the globe.

---

| | | |
|---|---|---|
| 1 BOTTLE RED | 1 cup CLUB SODA | 1 APPLE |
| 1/4 cup BRANDY | 1/4 cup ORANGE LIQUEUR | 1 PEAR |
| 2 tbs SUGAR | 1 LEMON | 1/2 cup POM SEEDS |
| 1 ORANGE | 1 LIME | 2 CINNAMON STICKS |

---

In a large pitcher, combine orange, lemon, and lime slices along with the apple and pear wedges, pomegranate seeds, and cinnamon sticks. Pour in the brandy, orange liqueur, and sprinkle with sugar. Add the bottle of red wine and gently stir the ingredients to combine and help dissolve the sugar. Refrigerate the sangria for at least 4 hours, or overnight, to allow the flavors to meld. The longer it sits, the more the fruit and cinnamon will infuse the sangria. Just before serving, top the sangria with sparkling water or club soda for a festive fizz. Garnish with fresh rosemary sprigs to add a touch of Christmas greenery. Serve in wine glasses over ice.

# Vino

## 'Tis the Seasonal Mulled Wine

The Romans credited for pioneering the practice of heating wine and infusing it with spices. As the Roman Empire expanded, so too did the popularity of this spiced wine, adapting to local tastes and ingredients across Europe. The concept of mulled wine evolved over the centuries, particularly in medieval times when it was believed to promote health and ward off sickness. Today, mulled wine is synonymous with winter and Christmas festivities, celebrated in many cultures for its warmth, rich flavors, and ability to bring cheer to the cold months.

---

| | | |
|---|---|---|
| 1 BOTTLE RED | 8 WHOLE CLOVES | 1 ORANGE |
| 1/4 cup BRANDY | 3 CINNAMON STICKS | 1/2 tsp NUTMEG |
| 1/4 cup SUGAR | 3 STAR ANISE | |

---

In a large pot, combine all ingredients. Start with the wine, then add the brandy, sugar (sub with honey if desired) orange slices, cloves, cinnamon sticks, star anise, nutmeg — you can also add cardamom pods and cranberries if you want. Gently warm the mixture over low to medium heat. It's important to avoid boiling, as this can cook off the alcohol and alter the flavors. Aim for a gentle simmer. Let the wine simmer for at least 15 minutes to allow the flavors to meld together. You can simmer for up to 3 hours, depending on how strong you'd like the spice flavors to be. Be sure to keep the heat low and cover the pot if simmering for longer periods. Once the mulled wine is flavored to your liking, strain out the spices and orange slices. Serve the wine hot in mugs or heatproof glasses. Garnish each glass with a fresh orange slice and a cinnamon stick.

# Shopping List

# Shopping List

www.ingramcontent.com/pod-product-compliance
Lightning Source LLC
LaVergne TN
LVHW070141110826
845147LV00002B/303

* 9 7 8 1 9 6 2 3 7 2 6 2 6 *